Ideas of Improvisation

Joel Dias-Porter

Published by Thread Makes Blanket
www.threadmakesblanket.com

Thread Makes Blanket titles are
distributed by AK Press

first edition

ISBN 978-0-9897474-6-2

Cover Design by Josh MacPhee
Interior Layout by Hyacinth Schukis
and Marissa Johnson-Valenzuela

Printed in Canada

I first read "El Magnifico" in a prison cell in Virginia, and in twenty years of re-reading the poem I've never not wept. That a man who called himself DJ Renegade could do that, writing about a baseball player I'd never heard of, introduced me to a different way to twist loss into beauty. *Ideas of Improvisation* is an exponent of the music and wonder and noticing that somehow *hit me like the flat end of a bat* and warmed me like the best of brown liquors. There are poetry collections, & then there's the gathering together of all things that matter into a single volume. Improv is the latter.
—Reginald Dwayne Betts

Reading Joel Dias Porter's *Ideas of Improvisation* is like listening to an album in which the singer extols the power of Black vernacular. These odes and elegies know more than what they say and say plenty as they take us through a history of America, of poetry itself, and even of math! This is a debut like no other . . . born of the time it takes to understand we're *more/ than the sum of what/ we've survived.*
—Jericho Brown

Joel Dias-Porter's poetic improvisations plumb the depths and scale the heights of personal narrative at the crossroads with a national narrative of Black sound and music. Here, he sings from the scarred and listing boat of collective desire and croons from the *bluest mountains of Duende.* Here he hollers Bebop in the hollows around a heart thick with prosody. Here you may behold the good sense of a *grasper of the chisel,/ caught in a wash to hammer it all*—that sings lifes' succulence and salvation—onto the page.
—Tyehimba Jess

CONTENTS

iii

Ideas of Improvisation

Joel Dias-Porter

RAP 23

a DJ Reneg8d remix

Say the Creator my OG,
so I can't be caught short.
Say they hip me when to chill in the park
and when to cool out by the river.
They school me with knowledge of self
and keep me doing the right thing—to represent.
Then yo, even when I step through the shadows
of the buildings in the projects,
I ain't sweating it cuz they got my back.
They flex if suckers try to press
which helps a brotha roll unstressed.
So picture forehead kisses
and take home plates from cookouts
until I'm outta here,
and then me just chilling
at they vacation crib
forever.
Peace.

"i is the imaginary unit. Although there is nothing real with this property, i can be used to extend the real to what is called complex."

WHITMAN'S SAMPLER

a DJ Reneg8d remix

To begin with, take warning, I am . . .
far different from what you suppose;
I do not ask any . . . delight, I swim in it as in a **sea**.
Then the eyes close . . . and . . . speed forth to **the darkness**,
Mind not the old man beseeching the young man,
Entering but for a minute . . . see a sight beyond
all the pictures and poems ever made,
Ebb stung by the flow and flow stung by the ebb,
love-flesh swelling and deliciously aching,
Have you ever loved the body **of** a woman?
Have you ever loved the body of a man?
O I think it is not for life I am chanting . . . my chant of lovers
         . . . it must be for death . . .
The sniff of **green leaves** and dry leaves, and of the shore,
and dark-color'd sea-rocks, and of hay in the barn;
And what I assume you shall assume;
Stop this day and night with me, and
you shall possess the origin of all . . .
In the mystical moist night-air, and from time to time,
Here, take this gift,
Which too long I was offering to feed my soul,
But I do not talk of the beginning or the end,
Stout as a horse, affectionate, haughty, electrical,
i and this mystery, here we stand.

AN IDEA OF IMPROVISATION AT 33 1/3 RPM

for Eardrum

Try holding **the** needle
      like a **lover's** hand
Or lowering it
      until it **tongues**
      the record's ear
Maybe cultivate
      what sweet beats bloom
      in the valley of the groove.
Let's laugh at folks
      that make requests
Because what Chef would allow
      diners to determine
Which entrees
      make up the menu?
Young cats
      dream about
      flashy flicks
      of the wrist
Yet what if it's about
      filling the floor
      with the manic language
      of dance
About ciphering the beat
      of every **rhyme**
      like a mama deciphers
      her child's cries?
What if nobody cares
      how fast you scratch
Because it isn't about
      soothing any itch
but about how many hairstyles
      are still standing
At the end of the night?

THE COLTRANE IN YOU

por il miglior fabbro

nightly probes
the first oh
of whatever emotion
your dark matter
splays open.
Meaning inky-haired
& lightheaded,
you trace
a circle at your center
pondering if
in a reunion
of broken things
the Beloved might be
Euler's Identity.
Meaning since the tint
is at least half the sound
and apostasy can loiter
on the tongue as a lozenge,
you seek to phrase
which shade of faith
versus gothic of god
might serve more
than mere ode or elegy.
Meaning at the wheel
of the warship of worship
you vie for the root of unity
to unravel extended chords
and strive to maroon
in the bluest mountains
of duende.
Meaning certain starred charts
—once incomplete—
may become guide

in a bitter suite
as incensed ropes of smoke
muscle music from hunger
—also known as splay—
how want preys
to probe
the pouty mouth
of imagination
or queries the angel
and lion of Evangelion
if the same L
that links them—
archaic name
for god or
vernacular for loss—
also superposes the word
in the world.
Meaning what if
the "good news" concludes
the Beloved is Apophenia?
Since all musicians
learn at least twelve ways
to kneel and kiss the ground,
surely the second O
of said emotion
could mean all things
in modulation,
perhaps how to be drawn
around a circle of fifths
or better Picasso keys
into a piano's grand motif?
Maybe re-choir
the Acknowledgement
of our father?
Meaning a relative minor
to greater absolve

any resolve for Resolution
or a full-hipped logic
to Bearden the burden
of our double basis
until battered sticks shatter
and every Zildjan
begins to shiver
into symbols brushed
by the breadth
of our questions.
Meaning a talent
may also be a weight,
thus your gift gives pause—
purpling in turbulent
Pursuance of relief,
wind from a box
spilling uncertain **bottled spirits**
—*e pluribus unum*—
as if God was an American
Sonnet massaged
into the Psalms
of Wanda's hands.
Meaning what
of this gift—
this **prayer**—
this petition signed
by two lips
bobbing about
a Brooks theory
of the Lyric
between lines
that twist
to conflate or conflict
until they feel
wholly writ?

AN IDEA OF IMPROVISATION WITH THE UNCERTAINTY PRINCIPLE—Take X

a free jazz of ashes buried or scattered by a ¿dead? cat in a different key

which **perhaps** could appear
—beloved—as points
on the musical taste
of The Black Raspberries,
although **the** shrubs might be
mostly bladed petals and
it was quite a pinch
when a **light** note later
the tax purposes **of** thorns
entered us for the first time
via a Pointillist painting
of **a pond** that sounded
tailored in the moment by Cecil
pleating some fundamental theorem
of jazz *i* hadn't fathomed,
yet heard again and again
beyond the decaying
of those phrases
or **the** raspy syntax
which Apophenia—
our anagogic diva—
might've brayed or splayed,
maybe to **diagram**
for religious reasons
as *The Drunken Garden*,
but perhaps merely to venture in
or splinter out until
some **feeling almost** inspires*
a round of blade-dancing
raised up to **the point of**
a sound science.

WEDNESDAY POEM

With duplicate poems and Xeroxed **desire**
to seed our students with **the** bloom
and oblivion of the ***Wild Iris***, Coates and I
clear the metal detector **inside** Cardozo High.
We bop down two long flights of steps
before scribbling our names in a logbook, but
just outside the classroom something feels
too quiet. Mr. Bruno (who's Boriqua and writes
poems) takes maybe ten minutes to open
the familiar door. There's something in his hand,
a snapshot. Remember Maurice Caldwell?
He didn't come to class much. Now, he won't
be coming at all. A Crisis Response Team
calls the kids like darting birds into a circle.
Every computer in the room seems blank.
Taped to the dry surface of the blackboard is a sketch
of Maurice, pinned below it, a bouquet of cards.
Keisha (who writes funny poems) says Maurice
would help her with Math, she liked him but
never said so. The Crisis lady says, "It's OK to cry."
Keisha says, "We been ran out of tears."
Mr. Bruno adds, "Somebody called him
from a car parked on Thomas Place NW.
When he walked up, they fired three times."
I freeze, that's barely a half block from my crib.
I don't remember if there are three or four crack houses
on that block. I walk through the low shrubs of that street
almost never. Why'd he approach the waiting car,
was he hustling Love Boat, crack or weed? Now
his face flashes before my irises, *i* see him horseplaying
with Haneef, his hair slicked back in a ponytail.
He wrote one poem this entire semester, maybe,
a battle rap for cartoon characters. Mr. Bruno asks
if we'll still teach, I open my folder of green poems,

then thumb each page with a dry purpose. Parliament
Funkadelic once sang "Without humps there'd be no getting
over" but what dark earth could these pistils protect?

AN IDEA OF IMPROVISATION ON THE LIBERTY BRIDGE

Say Emily, my piano playing better half
sporting cat glasses and a floral sundress
bent to sniff a bundle of fresh daisies before
dashing across a bridge—frfr—just as my
iPod cued Ahmad Jamal's cover of "Wave."
Both a wave and a tear can be falling water.
A wave can be water or a flag rippling. Some
flags can be read. And surely as the Em Dash
is named for Dickinson, before wrestling with
her texts, maybe I needed an ESL course:
Emoji as a Second Language. Perhaps she fled
because I couldn't tell the difference between
semaphore & metaphor or perhaps because
I couldn't play a more dominant chord,
or perhaps she simply longed for the longer
fingers of a pianist to key the silent C
of her efflorescence. Maybe you've already
read about how I allegedly gave her a ring
of rust on the windowsill of her heart, or how I
failed to see Emily could begin with the number *e*
or how soon afterwards I perhaps crossed north
over a cantilevered bridge in May to toss a bouquet
of daisies into the Monongahela. Say certain
things accumulated a few scents toiling overtime
in the olfactories, couldn't a fine pollen have
also briefly finessed a sneeze? My Beloved
fled just as Jamal began fingering falling water.
And here I should be frank, right? Forget that,
perhaps it's not true, but let's say I misread Emily
due to the wavy sines piercing my ears. Say,
in place of her neck I nosed a bottle-blue scarf
she'd left on the arm of a sofa. A steel cantilever
here only holds up reality. In green truth, I didn't

15

smell farewell until she high-heeled out the door.
As she sliced up the street, **late sunlight** buttered
her path and I finally began to believe in God
as perhaps metaphor or sugar pill. I still couldn't
imagine tears as more than waves of salt water
under the bridge of my glasses. Did Emily not beg
us to "dwell in possibility"? Maybe *i* just imagined
a Bill Evans tune spanning keys like **crow's wings**
darkening the day's eye until my heart gave out
a refrain that rhymes with **the** fragrance of **daisies** . . .

AN IDEA OF IMPROVISATION WITH PTSD

Piano Trumpet Sax Drums
Peyote Trazadone Sinsemilla Demerol

In a bus station bathroom, scribbled
initials trigger kisses on a nipple
or a needle's pulse through an arm—
but if—for religious reasons—you lick
these fingers can you taste my assault or
the grain *i* pearled into a luminous shell?
What else might color a domain
in the hippocampus or paper over
a toilet's oval as I tongue a girl named
Apophenia like a Percocet and perhaps
the documentary could be soundtracked
by plunging syringes or trigger clicks
but who blessed high startle reflex or
terror from nowhere waiting for a bus?

Piccolo Tambourine Synth Duduk
Pulse Tremor Seizure Dementia

Even as sum of what's been done to you
are there wholes in your search history?
Do you miss when a buss didn't mean kiss
when fingers didn't trigger unasked touch
or arrive as an **evening** express to shame
until the Speaker desires to disembark
or blow like **smoke** into a parallel reality
where **the sages** are more than mere apes
with a **vocabulary** & a rational capacity?
Why do some memories keep extending

like 4 cords blending into an encore
by the band Cycling Back To The Seen,
who sometimes warn about night sweats
but never about how the bus hits you?

FATHER, SON AND THE HOLY GHOST

We pray mainly in the alleys of memory.
There, shards of smiles glitter the ground, **but**
here we wear—almost—identical names
as scars, though **you** won't or **can't** remember
what date I was born. Something trickles down
the side of my face. **In some versions** this
may be all you have taught me: needles are
hollow lines which collapse as many families
as veins. Now **a** convict in **death**'s work camp,
you wither each day until **we may** count your
T-cells with one hand. When Mama's **voice** begs
from the phone "Please buy a dark suit to wear,"
i may be wrong—**but** I say **"Don't** some of us
wear black all day, everyday, anyway?"

AN IDEA OF IMPROVISATION AS THE CRY IN CRISIS

Jonathan said to David, Go in peace, for we have sworn friendship with each other in the name of the Lord . . .
–I Samuel 20:42

What if
from asylum
John begat a ballad
so upside-down
his sax curved into a question
marked by its mouthpiece—
why Dawn's fingers
might crack the sky's black shell
and the sun yoke itself
to a Beloved's promise—
a narrow riff of flaring rays
arrowing a b-flat until
it elides rails of scales
past time signatures
into a wilderness called Ziph
daring the curves
of a treble clef troubled
as imaginary numbers
or why fingers might ache
repressing the keys of a tenor
until perhaps he tongues
three notes as one
drop of sweat ripples his neck
or the sun cloaks him
in a psalm he could belt
with chords from David—
to a forbidden boy.

ELEGY INDIGO

The text for today is early Miles, the Columbia years . . .
That tone pared down to essentials.

   –Sekou Sundiata

"Did Miles mute his horn, because
breezes carry kites a gust might mutilate?"
Call him poet, professor. Call me grasper of the chisel,
caught in a wash to hammer it all.
Memories rush in, waves recede
like a blue crab across sand,
something bright clasped in each claw.

Finally, finally, I come to believe in loss as a way of knowing.

How long until one hears what silence can say?
I stand at a stoplight, waiting for colors to change.
At fifty-five one deals with eyesight fading.
Not as denim fades from knees of your favorite jeans
or lights fade on a stage above a microphone,
but how a goateed poet in a stingy brim hat
might fade the bets of a hooded man with holes for eyes
or scythes where fingernails should be.

Finally, finally, I come to believe in loss as a way of knowing.

If **the** Blues is a **river**, can't it carry in or wash away?
LEDs are replacing halogen and incandescent lamps,
so the headlights of some **approaching** cars are bluer
as his velvet rumble joins the voices of **my** fallen **fathers**.
And something trembles, ever so—a kite's tail in a breeze—
or the **shimmer** of a Harmon mute in the distance.

Finally, finally . . . I come to believe in loss as a way of knowing.

AN IDEA OF IMPROVISATION AT *PORTO INGLES*

As a boy I often went to the beach
beyond the schoolhouse to listen
to the dolphins chat with the whales
and watch the sails of boats
swell like the hanging shirts of men.
And how many whales still remain
from when my Papa left *Maio*
to hunt the oil in their heads for light?
The **smell of** whale oil tells me
there are more ways to burn
than there are for it to **rain**.
Some claim **the sea** is a stingy lover,
but maybe we just can't see her
returning rain **to** the sky.
Some might say she has harpooned
all five of my sons,
but they still **write** home.
Pasarinhu ki komi pimenta
sabi kel ku ki ten.
Because I never learned to read words
my wife Apofenia would decipher the letters,
but I can read the rocks **in a field**,
tell you whether to plant *midjo o nonsi.*
I have gone many years without my wife
as sometimes we go years without rain,
until the fields are scrimshawed
with as many bones as stones.
My bones converse more
on the coming of rain
than the man in the radio.
I like the man in the radio
because he doesn't insist
that everything stop while he talks.
This afternoon playing *oril,*

Antonio—who is from sunny cloud—
pointed out I can't drive a car,
but neither can he drive a burro.
He jokes that I'm salty because
I've never left *Maio,*
he believes there are flowers beyond
this island that I'll never see.
There are two things
I know for sure,
some people believe in no god
except the idea of god,
and here on *Maio*
we have more rocks
than flowers—
you don't water rocks
but neither do they die.
Sometimes I sit
and listen to the **waves**
until **the sun dips**
into the sorrow of the sea.
People always ask
how I've lasted
nearly one hundred years,
all I can say is—
"Konbersa sabe
e ladron di tempu."
This hat shades my face
as it shaded my father's,
but the light feels different,
maybe because some of it
now comes through wires.
Whales couldn't fit in the wires
and now their **song** is almost gone.
On these islands we have plenty light,
if you want to impress me,
make it rain.

IDEIAS DI IMPROVASON NA KRIOLU

konxa na praia—
tudu kuzas
nu ka ta sabe

shells on a beach—
all of the things
we don't know

txoro di gongon—
tudu rason
ela ka podi obi

gongon cry—
every reason
she can't hear

Manecon
na lingua di mudjer
fogo

Manecon
in (on) a woman's tongue
fogo (fire)

Morna—
azul di mar
ka sima azul di seu

Morna—
the blues of the sea
are not the blues of the sky

manxi—
odju di gintxu
mais bermedju

dawn—
the eye of the bird
more red

lua meia—
beju na orédja
dipos meia noti

half moon—
a kiss on the ear
past midnight

konxa na bu orédja—
mezmu ki mar
sodadi di mar

conch to your ear—
even at the ocean
longing for the ocean

txeru di txuba—
verdadi verdi
na janela

smell of rain—
green truth
through a window

THE BASHŌ IN YOU

green pistachios
half opened
snack girl's eyes

pearl earring
left in your lobe—
day moon

horse room—
your ponytail shakes
my apology

cowrie shell
among dreadlocks
the North Star

August heat—
the kink of the rope
between your teeth

your morning **grin**—
blackberry brandy
in breakfast tea

AN IDEA OF IMPROVISATION AS *MORNA*

Nearly every night I slip into a slumber
deep as the harbor of *Sao Vicente*,
chasing the fragrance of a woman
whose footprints fall like *txuba*
on the dry sand of my dreams.
Say her lips are bold as *badiu di Santiago*,
eyes green as the trees of *Santo Antao*,
hair black as the back beaches of *Fogo*,
picture brown skin as the hills of *Sao Nicolau*.
All her teeth glistening white as *Sal*,
fingernails neat as the streets of *Maio*,
perhaps a pout round as *Boavista*,
legs slender as *Santa Luzia*,
or two feet tiny as *Brava*.
Who wouldn't wish to sunbathe on her beach,
while the white tips of waves lick their legs
with water warm as fresh milk,
palm trees dance in a breeze
and **an airplane** pulls a white thread
through the sky's blue silk?
Just once, let her *Kriolu* tongue
be a sliver of sugar cane
between my lips.
But the Atlantic hisses like a jealous hag,
insists **these islands** are only
ten pimples on a vast face.
A heart skips quick as a *koladera*,
why can't these be West Africa's fingertips
reaching for America,
reaching for me?
Tonight, **the moon** rises shiny
as the underside of a tuna,
an evil *i*, it gazes
with a lunacy tireless as the tide.

Seagulls become questions gliding
through a mind.
Tell me Luna, how far
can one trace footprints
through a dream's shifting sand?
My pen ploughs crooked lines
across a barren page,
plants brown stanzas
into terraces up the hillside
of something like hope.
The branches of all the trees
seem to bend in the direction
of answers to a different question—
What small animal hasn't run
on or from something
rabid as desire?

BETCHA BY GOLLY WOW

for Phyllis Hyman

What blue wail is this, whose child so alone
their tasseled scarf of tightly knit notes
trails to caress green hills past dusk[1]? Or quotes
lush echoes, bouncing like balled fists off stone
faces that flail or float in Southside streams,
warning throats to beware their half-sipped woes.
Pulling bipolar box cars in their flow,
exiting St. Clair Village under steam[2].
Phyllis, how **your lips** once puckered with flair,
barely brushing our **naked** neck most nights
with lace feathers of whistled melody
rippled out of **June rain**. What splits our air
daring still to dip or flutter[3]? Whose kite
straining at its cord, dying to twist free?

---

1   June darkness fireflies pulse into police lights
2   last train her mascara still running
3   on the shoulder of the pallbearer a butterfly

AN IDEA OF IMPROVISATION WITH VIOLIN AT AN ANIMAL SHELTER

(which wasn't a moment of silence for Elijah McClain)

STILL LIFE
in chalk on asphalt

```
                 y          August cloud burst
streetlamps      e             between
blinking         l             raindrops
                 l             gunshots
                 o                              crows
brother          w                              staggering
(not here)                                      a power line
spilling     t
wine         a          Our father
             p          (who is Art                        A
Mary         e          in heaven)        light            M
  J                                       flashes           B
weeping.            white              a                    E
telling      b      outline    EMT     kind                 L
Martha       l      of         on      of                   A
             o      a          knees   hope                 M
             w      rigorous                                P
a girl       i      argument                               S
rapping      n
silence      g             Undercover
around                     copping
her              i
                 n      S
                        Q
                        U              naked
                 a      A              black
petals                  D              as fault
falling                                             S
on a             h      C                           Q      the
wet              u      A                           U      sound
black            n      R                           A      of
boy              g                                  D      red
                 r                                         in
                 y              puddle of           C      the
a single verb                  break fluid[1]       A      rain
an eight-sided                                      R
red sign         w
                 i
                 n
liquor           d                          fallen leaf
bottle                                    what's left of
cracking                                  my cool brown
up
```

"The narrative I too may bloom
as iris in the mason jar of the imaginary."

AN IDEA OF IMPROVISATION WITH RUMBLING CLOUDS

Say
Buffalo **buffalo** buffalo
do
Buffalo **buffalo buffalo** buffalo
until
Buffalo **buffalo buffalo buffalo** buffalo?

ALBEIT FOR G.S.

. . . only because
it was a Thursday
(which is her Monday),
and I thought she was walking
as though hauling something
heavy (yet not **in her hand**s),
and maybe *i* saw her sigh,
and so recalled Lonnie
(who you might not know)
not Lonnie who was always
pawning **his wedding band**
so he could feed the penny slots
or Lonnie from The Hill
who always seemed to be
half a slice short of a sandwich,
but Lonnie from *"Lonnie's Lament"*
(and here she cocks her head and
wrinkles her nose saying "Who?")
because whatever could **slant**
his **rain** so sideways
perhaps allowed Coltrane
to raise a sax to his lips
and blow a lamentation
as her Monday motion,
a wistful wisp of piano
nearly legato as her legs,
or a bassline
of hair that plunges
when she brushes it
into a black Niagara,
which she can't know
may convince me
I could spend

the rest of my days
naked and trembling
in a maple barrel,
falling forever
into its obsidian mist.

AN IDEA OF IMPROVISATION AS COMPULSIVE PRAYER

What's the difference between chocolate and any other desire darkened? Or pray tell which need registers deepest in a casino—those giant shrines to Apophenia—where a man who wagers by probability and therefore can't be addicted encounters the Incompleteness Theorem of a woman who dips to serve him dissolved spirits? Is it the vagus nerve which makes the octaves of chocolate in her skin french horn into harmony in the music hall of his mouth? If—and only if—you've ever wagered and lost it all, then you might grasp why a choir means to gather, yet still not guess what it means to hymn. Could we still pretend that the phattest asymptote isn't objective reality if Schrödinger's Equation uses the square root of minus one or if any door besides endorphins swings our hunger to spinning numbered wheels? Is said door mascara **black** or **lipstick** red? Is this the part of the arc where we deduce free will is an illusion, yet sit undecided if our gambler's luck means Schrödinger's cat will be black as **a clarinet** strung around Rahsaan Roland Kirk's neck? Or where he compounds his loss by counting **her** name in red as a **rosary** he may need the darkest chocolate to unlearn?

THE BUKOWSKI IN YOU

after Terrance Hayes

What else is left
if your last stack of chips
gets shipped the other way
and your mouth gapes
wide as the wallet
of a man snoring
on a park bench—
but to limp out and
return to the shadows
of a waiting tomb
before curling up like
the last piece of pasta
on a paper plate?
Now even the women
sweeping under oval tables
and trashing styrofoam odors
may not brush you
into their dusty pans.
The red deck, the blue deck,
the shuffle machine,
all reduce you
to a splotch under
the dealer's manicured nails,
their Rolex stopped to watch.
Damn. Damn. Damn.
Everything you touch stutters.
You can't recall
how singing sounded
before the Ace of Hearts
collapsed your last lung,
can't feel your buddy
tapping your shoulder,
frowning "Just take the loss."

You flash back to the rising
ride to your room,
39 floors of sunk stomach
before the floral scowl
of a used towel
across the bathroom floor.
Suppose you were nothing
but that hand towel
in a $49 motel?
Suppose you lived
to lick beads of brightness
from **a** working **girl's**
pimpled back,
but all you had
were parched **lips**
and a swollen tongue?
Suppose **you** still **pretend**
not to see in the cards
how Apophenia
is the massage girl of god?
Maybe that's how **whiskey**
soaks into the casks,
slight burn in the beginning,
then oak smooth and
polished as a casket,
or why when
the River card rises,
whatever you feel
is hollow tipped as a bullet.
More so if you dig
digging in moist soil.
Even more so, if
you're not a gardener
or a man in a ball cap
wanding the beach for beeps.
Admit at least

how you're drawn
to the gutbucket dance
of the blue deck,
or to the way
the red deck
teases like a pair
of painted toes.
Perhaps you're addicted
to a feeling that even
a storefront psychic
can't peep in your cards,
no matter how far
she pursues
the balsa grooves
of either palm.
Perhaps you're committed
to denying how cards
mostly dream of the digits
they aren't dealt to.
What could be sexier
than the way
desperation's red dress
hugs her hips?
Is that why you
buy back in,
why you tease
your rolling chair
to the table's edge
and post a blind bet—
why you peel the corners
of your hole cards
like they're prosperity's
last pair of good panties?

AN IDEA OF IMPROVISATION WITH THE TABLE OF CONTENTS OF *THE HUMAN HOURS*

The amenities -- En route -- An apprehension -- The skin of the face is that which stays most naked, most destitute -- The light from **across** the **fields** -- Forensics -- Still life -- Epistemology -- Landscape with borrowed contours -- Lyric and narrative time at Café Loup -- Appeal to numbers -- Accursed Questions, i -- Comic morning -- Idée fixe -- Essay on An essay concerning human understanding -- Lore -- Son in August -- The necessary preoccupations -- The art of the security question -- O Esperanza! -- Accursed questions, ii -- The humanities -- Calamity Jane on Etsy after the 2016 election -- Let facts be submitted to a candid wind -- Another Divine comedy -- Metaphor on the Crosstown -- The **sky flashes** -- Summons -- Origin story -- Central Park -- Accursed questions, iii -- Pain scale -- 433 Eros -- In the studio at end of day -- Uncertainty principle at the Atrium Bar -- Beckett on the Jumbotron -- Uncertainty principle at **dawn** -- **Prayer** for the lost among us -- The material world -- Eternal recurrence -- Accursed questions, iv -- Amor fati.

SEASCAPE WITH VESSEL

for Cesária Évora

Tonight **at** the end of a bar,
at **the end of a woman's cigarette**,
a voice hums what feels
like Melancholy's middle name.
Consider **the** amber **mystery**
of a Single Malt timbre
rising like a *Tchintchirote* over waves.
And why with the ease of **a girl**
rinsing sea salt from her hair,
or the rhythm of a boy
kicking rolled up socks,
said voice might hint at *Frutu Proibido*
known only to the night,
or *Destino Negro* drawn in the stars.
Yes, some may grumble
it gambled its gift like a pack of Marlboros,
but what sun doesn't exhaust itself nightly
in the offing?
Perhaps our siren has elided,
but not before the *bentu lestri*
tries to whisper why
its melody could remain
moist as sand after the sea's kiss.
Why even if a cold breeze
pimples our tongues
outside a bar *na terra lonji*
Sodade, Sodade might return us
to those ten rugged rocks
wrinkling the aqua silk of the sea . . .

EL MAGNIFICO

Who am I?
I am a small point in the eye of the full moon
I need only one ray of the sun to warm my face
I need only one breeze from the tradewinds to refresh my soul
What else can I ask, if I know that my sons really love me?

                                        –Roberto Clemente

Even under a heavy quilt,
there's a breeze
from a distant
transistor radio.
My lips mimic
a slice of honeydew
as they remember
it's New Year's Day—
the last before heading
back to school.
Straining to hear the broadcast
above my brother Jeff
snoring in the bunk below,
I roll over.
The regular program
has been interrupted
by **the sound of** waves
washing against a shore
which I pretend is
not my mother **praying**.
It's January in Pittsburgh,
which is to say
the radiator shudders
against what howls
outside **our** cracked **window**.
After hopping down onto cold linoleum,
and tiptoeing to Mama's bedroom door,
I cup one ear

to the plies of wood.
The radio reports that a plane
flying Roberto Clemente,
food, and clothing
to earthquake victims in Nicaragua,
is missing off the coast of San Juan.
No bodies have been located,
only debris bobbing in the waves.
The words hit my chest
like the fat end of a bat.
I collapse at the base
of the door
until my mother cracks it—
her own eyes raw—
and picks me up
rocking slowly.
A glove left
in the Little League grass
is all I knew of loss.
Even though a stadium shouting
Arriba Roberto
was all I knew of *español*,
didn't I fall asleep most nights
pretending he was my father?
In our world of chipped asphalt
and falling bricks,
his John Henry swagger
was perhaps all I knew of myth.
Hadn't *i* taken a black crayon
and drawn the number 21
on the back of a T-shirt,
then raced to play right field
because his glove upturned
for a basket grab
was all I knew of grace?
Brown as spiced rum,

blacker than barges of coal,
he somehow covered the gap
between Puerto Rico's cane fields
and our three rivers.
Dark smoke choked the sun,
our city of rusty bridges and rolling hills
began to lose the glow from its fabled mills.
And on a rocky Puerto Rican shore,
his family gathered to hymn
as waves peaked into shark's teeth
and the arms of palm trees swayed
Adios Roberto, Arriba.

AN IDEA OF IMPROVISATION ON SILENT NIGHT

As a little kid,
i loved how the Allegheny County Jail
resembles a castle,
but now I've come to visit
the only man I've ever kissed on the lips.
The sun has retired,
the wind cuts like razor wire
as snowflakes float above
its stone walls.
I follow Mom through
the doorway of a metal detector,
produce proper ID,
and submit to searching hands.
The visiting room is thick
with cigarette smoke.
Collated into stalls, women
hunch under a heaviness
of words, each syllable
a bubble in a stew.
Inside the control booth,
a guard's electric eyes
squint to an empty cubicle
with two chairs.
The steel bars buzz,
and my father steps through
in a pressed **prison jumpsuit**
his lips forced into a smile.
Track marks
show why he avoids
short sleeves.
Mom cradles the phone,
almost whispering.
Despite months of unpaid child support
why does **his last paycheck** wait

in her purse to bail him out
on our first Christmas
together as a family?
Weren't the bleachers always blank
when I played Little League?
Isn't what I want most for my birthday
simply for him to remember it?
By my turn on the phone the air is polarized.
Our gazes cross like sabers.
I pretend to study the wires
crissing across the thick glass,
then eye the shoelaces I deliberately left untied.
But the man who assembled my first model plane,
who taught me to shoot a jumper,
whose charcoal sketches I copied,
is caged with a number on his chest.
His jokes bounce off the barrier between us.
Questions streak their gray fingers through his hair.
"Are you in the tenth or eleventh grade now,
did you make the chess team again?"
He claims to be learning to play.
When he complains about the **prison food**
before asking what Mom fixed,
I describe even **the cranberry sauce**
sliced into a roll of red coins.
The clock munches minutes.
A knot in my throat
stops me from *I miss you*,
or *How much longer?*
Instead I mumble about
the Steelers chances in the playoffs.
The guard signals and we rise,
as I reach my new height,
he stands up in surprise.
He seems shorter now,
but still manages to say

"I know being here
must be difficult for you, son
Try not to give your mother a hard time, OK?"
When he leans forward
the window's clouded pane
captures a print of his lips.
I nod my head.
The C.O. turns a key
to slide the bars aside.
As he turns I grip the phone,
eyes glistening—
but wait until
his footsteps fade—
before pressing my lips
to the glass.

THE BARTHES IN YOU

Apophenia as signifier

in molecular letters

by a drunken tattoo, not

in scanned lines of prosody

of Whiskey Foxtrot Tango?

not loud, proud or merry

sines of a sampling machine

as a cosine of its own wend.

or sum unrequited subtext

stated symbolically

a tavern cryptograph ~ a bar code

{Sin, NECK, Dough, Key}

Perhaps 8:08 as heartscape

until Roland on a river triggers

or metonymy's tangent

AN IDEA OF IMPROVISATION WITH BLACK GRANITE

for Rob and Denise

As when we almost
at a red light
decided to veer west on Constitution Ave.
away from a white quilt of tourists
before coursing
like blue-black threads
right through them.
Or when you and Denise query
what I recall of the war.
An old TV screen humming
with helicopters,
or two men, maybe, emerging
from a green tangle of leaves.
How they carried a bandaged comrade
the way I carry my father's first name,
but never—it seems—
his blessing
or how a Buddhist monk
reposed in robes
a darker orange than
the gasps which engulfed him.
Are we ever **old** enough
to grasp a flame's greed?
All conversation seems to fade
as we near the Book of Names.
I read Robert Louis Howard,
Panel 22W,
but you whisper "Thua Thien,
June 1969."
We turn the corner
to the **headstone** of an era,
a funeral without end.
Is the sudden reign of **silence**

reverence or shame?
Wreaths, carnations and roses
echo against the stone,
as heads bow.
A legless vet rolls by,
and I nearly blame the eye
of a camera for blinking.
Your Pop's name floats
thirteen lines from the top.
As the tallest, I square **the** rectangle
then begin to shade.
After the first trace of his **name**,
the arithmetic hits me—
the summer of '69
found you in diapers.
All you've ever had
for a father
is a Sergeant's smile
on a curling Polaroid
and a tri-folded flag.
i promised not to tell
if the reflecting pools
of our eyes began to fill,
but one of us crumpled
with a letter that vexes still.
Why? We make it
to nearby benches
on the verge of splinters—
then begin to hug and rock
as Denise starts to hum;
"Hush now, don't explain . . ."
Above us
a flag with stripes
redder than even
our eyes.
Below us,

the white silence
of three tight-lipped
bronze soldiers.
Above that,
an August sky
almost blue
as the tremble
in Denise's contralto.

SOLO IN THE KEY OF NICOLE

Not just because Miss Sweet Potato Brown
      —a mini cocoa statuette—
felt conflicted as flecks of Chet
      baked in the **almonds** of her eyes.
Or because I refused to admit
      that after kissing her and tasting stars
      i stumbled into drugstores
      and slowly undressed
      some of the chocolate bars.
Not because her cayenne tongue twirling
      set beige rooms whirling
her jet tresses swirling
      so devilishly dervish
and nonsensically nervous
      yet crayon scribbles
      on a Scrabble board weird.
Or because she babbled against roses
      and wouldn't hold hands
      yet napped in my cashmere sweater
      as an omen against the cold.
But perhaps because after cups
      of Raspberry tea I spied
      in the sugar bowl of **her smile**
as she cut the deck in quarters
      and dealt Hearts to all the chairs
the face up cards still felt as if
      she was playing Solitaire . . .

AN IDEA OF IMPROVISATION WITH THE YOU IN NOCTURNE

for Yen

Heart-taker,
I have always loved
to say "acetaminophen,"
even before I knew
if it rhymed
with the electric
currency of your name
or the crescent face
of another woman
appeared to warn
some words could twist
into the darkness
of nibs of licorice.
Unlike your name
acetaminophen isn't
a shadow-colored word
pitting spots of Sriracha
on the white cloth of silence,
although both have
been known to raise
a man's blood pressure
like the top of Schrödinger's box.
I still dream of some words
Swedish massaging
knots of my heart,
while others
like "acetaminophen,"
sharpen into steel swords
drawing blood.
Your name—
a nocturnal hum—
a lunar pill in a language

not under my tongue.
Old men who draw thin
in poker games
act as if Hope
never becomes
habit forming.
A Knave of Hearts,
i may have been seen
licking its stains
from both lips while
attempting to smile
in neurotypical.
Did Hafez not write
that the gnarly roots
of hope
might be boiled
into an extract
to alleviate
even the **barking cough**
of loneliness?
Some nights my bark
is a listing boat,
other nights
an overcoat.
Because your eyes
sometimes seem dotted
as the I's
of **an** expired **prescription**,
my cheeks still seek
to rhyme
with acetaminophen.
Perhaps this simply
lacks a calculus
of lavender,
but tonight
would even the white pill

of **the moon**
be found in the mouth
of a man kneeling
to lift the weight
of your name
until light?

RADIO MALI AMERICAN GOTHIC BLUES

for Gordon Parks and Ali Farka Touré

Tell us please, where the learning tree grows,
If its branches row the sea to Timbuktu,
If its leaves shade both lensmen and griots?

Malcolm X in his fury, "The Greatest" in repose,
Even beggars in Paris your lens would not refuse.
Tell us once again where the learning tree grows.

The source of the Sahara as a river you composed,
In the heart of the moon buds **a branch** of brothel blues.
Do its leaves shade both lensmen and griots?

Your limbs bend from **the weight of** how many snows,
Yet, still your shutter scores with **moonlight** as its muse,
Tell us once again where the learning tree grows.

Baobab, your bark appeared to nurture poetry and prose,
Niafunké must've wailed as your falling broke the news.
How would your leaves shade both lensmen and griots?

Black and shining seem the feathers of a thousand crows
Who alight and fill the sky with their darkening news.
Do they grasp where the branches of the learning tree grow,
And if its leaves shade both lensmen and griots?

THE AL-KHWARIZMI IN YOU

graphs the slope
in your only child's eyes
into "Daddy when are you
coming back?"
Even before
he lays his head
on the hollow
around your heart
you try to recall the order
of operations for—
murmur
embrace
pout
dance
ask
sigh.
Although
he whispered
to you once—
·—his lips form
empty brackets now.
From this angle
the thesis of parenthesis
seeks to form
a transcendental equation.
You wonder if the idea
of all infinite series
is how father and son
might equal more than
the sum of what they survive?
Even for Khayyam or Clifford
what delta doesn't divide
Greek letters
on opposite sides

of said equation—
or italicize absence
by their presence?
Meaning aren't there **two halves**
to all mathematics:
the rules which we discover
& the set of symbols
we invent
to transcribe them?
The algorithms
governing distance
multiply in the abacus
of memory until
you begin to dream
of him whispering:
pear
endive
melon
date
apple
seaweed.
Could there be a calculus
for **the arc of** a ball
not tossed between you
and your boy—
for **the** arcs of hours
after the **divorce**
where you tried to solve
for the function of ex?
As the parent
in parenthesis
wouldn't you bend
every weekend
to kiss even the imagined
curve of his forehead?

THREE WRONG NOTES

Note the diameter of your invisible ink tattoo as if it hides
a crossword hint like "Clueless dope for dopamine"
But not because your inner twin sold all your rap albums
for a white powder that made you feel touched by God, yet
left a trail like Comet. Note how a certain name trails off with
the number *e* as if to signify their compound interest in
a continuously growing silence. Does an infinite series
of silences imply addition or addiction? In one language
you understand, *pegadu* means touching and begins with
the letter P. As Pi is filled with touches of fruitful irrationality,
and may hide a circle's private key. Note how rumors of you
crossing the street to sneak rides on fire trucks are irrational, but
not because you're vain or became a pyromaniac. The circumference
of urinal cakes may be solved with Pi or dissolved with pee.
Is it irrational that you looped like an extension cord while trying
to solve for the value of P, but got beat like a bowl of egg yolks
for wetting the bed? During the beating was their mouth *agápē* or
agape? Has it not been proven that trauma only feels transcendental
due to the ratio of the diameter which severs us to the circumference
which can make us feel whole? Note that the Sign of the Asp may be key,
but a volta sometimes turns as currents of a Ghanaian river
or in currents alternating like a weathervane until any cryptic tattoo
could simply signify who held you down and touched you, but also
told you to hold it forever because their love was like the Holy Ghost.

"Because where isn't the dot of the lyrical *i*
a pupil to the third I of improvisation?"

PORTRAIT OF THE AUTIST AS A STARFISH IN COFFEE

for Fritz, Harro, Ernst, and Hellmuth

Say your friend Gigi claims it may storm later,
but the primary aspects of your spectrum
are aspic, raspy, and aspirant. So perhaps you
beam an asparagus smile because your brain
just conjured up Oran "Juice" Jones singing
"I saw you (and him) walking in the rain."
Is this why Benjamin Franklin invented the internet
so that people could talk, but not face to face?
When you look at people you can read the ratios
in the bone structure beneath their skin, almost
the way other folk can read people's faces
like a vegan scanning a list of ingredients
but what if every expression was pimpled in Braille
and you had only catcher's mitts below your wrists,
or suppose when told to let sleeping dogs lie,
you wondered how a doberman could be dishonest?
Fact: The U.S. has over 95,000 miles of shoreline,
but on some plates the border between the country
of carrots and the province of peas will never meet—
let's say your brain is a **Pittsburgh bound train**
but your mouth is **a horse drawn Amish wagon**
and what dances **across** the stage of your cranium
isn't always projected on **the** scrim of your skin,
or your voice twists trying to **signal** "I believe you"
since she believes inflections the way Crayola
once believed in a peach crayon called "FLESH."
And maybe you can instantly multiply and divide
four or five digit numbers in your head, but
what if—for once—grasping a metaphor wasn't
like finding a formula to solve cube roots?
OK, perhaps Ben Franklin didn't exactly
invent the internet, but the internet does

contain pictures of him inventing electricity.
Fact: Pittsburgh has over 400 bridges,
most of which don't cross rivers, and say
she extends her hand to pat your arm
yet you jerk away because every finger
broadcasts a radiostatic charge, and alright
Ben Franklin didn't really invent electricity
but he certainly earned many pennies cutting
off lights during a thunderstorm,
so you try to stop to collect the new coins
of thought spilling from your pockets
even as you spot the pot on the back
of her electric range approaching a boil.
And we all know how you can hear even
incandescent bulbs like humming mosquitos
but as you attempt to read her tone spinning
like a Sinatra single on the platter of a Victrola,
Gigi just perplexes her head, peering
into your conch-like mouth as your arms
splay like a sea star mired in mocha sand
and her boat slowly begins to turn to steam.

SOMETIMES IT SNOWS IN APRIL

a DJ Reneg8d remix for LaSon C. White 1961-2007

April sprouts around us,
is the sky as sullen there? Wasn't
the hour after we talked
cruelest, most raw? In less than a
month, your oncologist says
breeding cells may overwhelm you.
Lilacs still bloom here as there, just
out screened doors. Hint
of all the Prince songs we share.
The purple petals nearly
dead certain to flurry down,
land and bury our walkways.

April's sibilant drizzle
is a ride cymbal mocking
the rhythm of memories,
cruelest at dusk. What other
month would dream of
breeding, then watering
lilacs as recent bruises?
Out of the patter
of the rain's fingers,
the alto vibrato of a voice
dead on key, humming "Adore",
lands on these ears.

April winds wane,
is that my ringtone amid
the evening news? No, it's on vibrate.
Cruelest is the quiet after the call.
Month after month will sprout,
breeding a grief fragrant as those
lilacs you adore. Because right now,

out on the horizon, the purple dirge
of a setting sun is perhaps
the last chance I'll have to be
dead silent and listen for you in the
land of the living.

ALGORITHM OF THE BLUES

Tonight, a needle dives
into a record's black skin
with the drive of a dove
winging against a window
and although this ain't
the ballad of a wounded bird
you may still pursue
in Charlie Parker's tone
new ways to phrase the moan
in "Testimony."
And listen—no matter
how high the moon—
could Bird ever transcribe
any dove's burden
with his knowledge
of "Ornithology?"
What else might lead Bird
to heat the bottle caps of chords
or push an arpeggio
into the whole of his hunger?
In some fashion
Bebop is nothing
he ever loved or nothing
that ever loved him,
just bright tones in a bandanna
tied across his brow.
But if one Missouri memory
hadn't slivered his lungs
would the Blues have tuned
the edge of his grin

to epistemology?
Joy says **birdsong** proves
the futility of words
because what human could improve
its contrafactual flow?
And some nights
even the moon takes notes
as Bird pecks a phrase—
fractures it—then flattens
& sharpens one eighth
into a swollen vein.
This paradox appears hypodermic,
a blue flame of bird-speak
underneath a spoon's black skin,
but let's say the song ain't over.
Some cats try to pull
from Parker's tone
as many parts wit as witness,
they insist the warp
and woof of the Blues
can weave bandannas
to flag down the yellow taxis
of axioms.
"BIRD LIVES"—they claim—
in this address of ghost notes
unexpected as ketchup
on corn flakes.
So you wait
still at the window
as he mines a horn's
phonographic memory—
which can't choose
what it does or doesn't save.
"Take a phrase
and fracture it"
they say

until you see how
some tunes might fray
into ontology.
Might bid one beg
a slender hand
to twist a band
into a bandage.

AN IDEA OF IMPROVISATION AT NEWPORT

a DJ Reneg8d remix

Bangles on bare arms and daisies on dresses,
Lip gloss that lingers and long sassy tresses,
Coltrane on track one and jingles that zing,
Lightning that hints at what evening might bring.

Raindrops paradiddle slick riddles
On our windshield, as I reach for
Roses O Beloved, which bend
And curl like your fingers through
Whiskers twisting into Farsi script
On a Sufi chin. Almost cryptic as
Kittens, droplets on the petals flash
Bright as halogen pin spots or mint
Copper pennies or Persian tea
Kettles kissed by candlelight.
And who wouldn't welcome this rain
Warm as your morning whispers, or
Woolen scarves or those cobalt
Mittens *i* wore last winter? Oh
Brown box of paraflex, oh folded
Paper lotus of hazel hands, twin
Packages of taffeta, soon to be
Tied down with joy's red ribbons. Listen
Up as rain's pitter aches to fill patterns
With knotty functions of leggy
String theory laced in fishnet. I've heard
These phrases Trane sometimes blazes
Are blessèd cries beyond any current Key:
A line nuzzled from Hafez ghazals or a
Few notes rising to float the bamboo span
Of a spine as menthol smoke or simply

My fingers' Morse code for their
Favorite shoulder blade inked with
Things soon to chrysalis and bloom.

Cranberry candles and cognac in crystal,
Satin pajamas and tongue tips that tickle,
Sweet tea from tumblers in summerlong swigs,
Church of dark chocolate, almonds and figs . . .

AN IDEA OF IMPROVISATION WITH THE UNCERTAINTY PRINCIPLE—Take Y

a free jazz of ashes buried or scattered by a ¿dead? cat in a different key

which might appear—
beloved—between points
on the musical taste of
The **Black Raspberries**,
or why I believed
the shrubs could be
mostly petals and
it was quite a pinch
when a grace note later
the tax purposes
of the horns pierced us
for the first time
via this Pointillist painting
of a pond tailored
in the moment
by Cecil pleating
some fundamental theorem
of jazz I couldn't
quite fathom,
yet heard **again and again**
beyond the decaying
of these phrases
or the gaspy syntax which
Apophenia—
princess of improvisation—
seemed to fray or splay
into hours to diagram
for science reasons
as a Quantum Garden,*

to venture in or enter out
until some desire required
a godly type of ghost note
i might believe in
mostly because
it was not . . .

SUBTERRANEAN NIGHT-COLORED MAGUS

theme & variations on a phrase from Amiri Baraka's "Wailers"

"Subterranean" as if
miles deep in a mine shaft
cored by minor intervals
or subtext rich as King Oliver's ore
bourn from the motherlode
maybe indigo undersongs
or seismic solos
on tectonic trumpet
or riffs down Richter's scale
til You're Under Arrest
spelunking funky rhythms
scaling Seven Steps to Heaven
or painting Sketches of Spain
all up under the canvas
til it bleeds
All Blues out the other side
dream the son of a dentist doing rootwork
with a hoodoo horn
hollering Bebop toasts
Petey Wheatstraw
Satchmo's son-in-law
or a signifyin junkie
trying to throw monkeys off his back
perhaps Shine below the Titanic's deck
blueing up its boilers
til he's blue like Bird
freight like Trane
early like Bird
night like Trane
wing like Bird
but railing like a Trane
rumbling underground.

"Night-colored" might be sable
as miles of tamped tarmac or
a nocturne rising on raven wings
jet in the sky Round Midnight
and yet an ebony kettle stewing
a Bitch's Brew
so black, it's **Kind of Blue**
think slick as black ice
cool as black snow
sweet as black cherries
on the Downbeat
like a blackjack
a black jackhammer
black Jack Johnson
black Jack
of all trades
digging down
past inkblack
purpleblack
oilblack
cinderblack
kohlblack
bootblack
to bottom of the hole black
Prince of Darkness
black tube tying off an arm
black ring
around **a woman's eye**
paving asphalt inroads
with your black turned to the audience
playing cooly under color of night.

"Magi" as in muted druid
of the blues
Traveling Miles
to follow charted stars
Miles in the Sky
Dark Magus? ask minders
of the metronome
say On The Corner
a soloing Sorcerer with E.S.P.
a jackleg preacher
testifying in a funky Tutu
not just 5,280 feet
climbing 1.6 klicks
in search of Amandla
but Live and Evil
whispering East St. Louie's Blues
yet In a Silent Way
cast Blue in Green spells
or cast a net of knotted cords
around Bag's Groove
say So What and hear Milestones
crash the stained-glass windows of jazz
have mercy, Man with a Horn
and make more joyful noises
rehearse your verses of Sufi Blues
running the Voodoo down
a circular scale as square roots
of negative notes
while we waif in this water
sacred dark and deep
with miles to go before we sleep
with miles to go before we sleep

SUNDAY POEM

for Ernesto, Brandon, Gary, and Reneé

Lilley and I discuss a famous poem
which claims "Death is the mother of beauty,"
walking up First St. NW, just before
the last streaks of sun leak from the sky
above Renée's crib where we hold
our Black Rooster workshop.
I recall holding Ronald
early one church morning after
he got shot on his Mama's front steps—
how his eyes rolled like white marbles—
and begin wondering if the same logic
which produced that poem,
also perhaps implied the mushrooms
that clouded Hiroshima or Nagasaki?
Someone yells from an idling green van,
we look over and it's Melvin who used
to have dreads and clown about "The Killer"
when he was **in** my WritersCorp **workshop**
at Lorton Prison. Only now he's free
and has shaved his head. The **light changes**
and Melvin pulls off, so I tell Gary
"The Killer" joke and we laugh so hard
I almost miss **the carnations** placed
by the stop sign, or the wine bottles
arranged around them like decorations
in a nigga cemetery. Gary
says "Damn" just as I peep the blown-up
photograph held to the fire-box
by maybe half a roll of Scotch tape.
And what does it mean that the name
"Pooh" is printed in blue ball-point above
a brother crouching as I once crouched
in nightclubs posing for five dollar pictures?

Perhaps I recognize this kid flossing
Nikes that match his Nautica jacket,
because I passed him or someone
similar to him coming out
of the liquor store on the corner
of Florida Ave last Friday, when I stopped
to cop a bottle of Evian and
some Juicy-Fruit. Their hair was cornrowed
and they cradled a beer in one hand,
while holding the door with the other.
And I pray *i* mumbled "Thanks," before the door
swung shut. There are two dates, neither
of which are dried fruit, scrawled under
the feet in the photo and I lean in to nose
one of the carnations. Now my eyelashes
clump as I recall stringing Ronald's
Nikes from the power lines above
his mother's crib. I pull my lucky geode
from a front pocket and set it down
near the bottles, then step back
under a sky that's gone all black
to ponder what Stevens might've written,
if the Beauty he so believed in
only sometimes believed in him.

THE MAN WITH THE [12 BAR] BLUES GUITAR

a DJ Reneg8d remix

Three

I & *i* sat [hat cocked] picking my guitar,
a traveling-man of sorts. The day seemed yellow.
They said, "You got a [delta] blues guitar,
can you play things colored as they are?"
I replied [Marlboro dangling], "Thangs
as they are, is hyacinth on a delta guitar."
And they said [Bible-eyed], "We want you to play,
a tune outside of us, but of yourself,
a [Gospel] truth on your blues guitar,
of things as a colored might feel they are."

Six

I never could hang a picture quite square,
although *i* tried to mojo it with care.
I don't try to sing a man's gold tooth
or linen suit, but his honeycreeper soul,
and eyes him down as well *i* can and picks
him up with my Mississippi hand.
When I plucks him up, moody as the moon
not sunlit like things as some say they is,
it becomes a trail of howl traveling far
from a Taurus that strums an acoustic guitar.

Nine

A ticking clock tune colored as we are,
somehow tinted by the [springstar] guitar;
ourselves [almost] humming as if on pitch,
and what's changed, except perhaps our faith
in things as they are and the meanings
as he bends them on the blues guitar,
stretched just so, the chords of change,
heard in a damned juke-joint;

for an moment damned, the way the hue
of hydrangea perhaps eternally sounds
where even the hand of god might be haze.
The blues can't stop time. And thusly [plucked]
seem the square root of a morning star,
the crossroads at midnight, but on a guitar.

Twelve

Are **these** [hellhound] blues merely mine?
Every devil of the delta thrives on **six strings**
to fill the [smoky] juke-joint with dancing women
in thrall with the moon. But **the** yellow-eyed men
of the women are [moody] blue, and soon coming
for only my [middle-parted] head that seldom **lies**
alone at night.* *i* fingers a string of cornflowers.
How to change the arrangement as it is? And how
as **I** frets these changes, to maybe **tune** my guitar
so it might distill an [eternal] tonic, and yet,
not bottle it. Could the blues be anything else?

A THEORY OF LYRIC

Harmolodics is how
a crow could've once been
improvised from chromium,
oxygen, and tungsten.

—Ornette Coleman (probably)

IRONY OF A NEGRO ARTIST

for Jean-Michel Basquiat

Become a star Famous Negro Artist Learn to Repel Ghosts

Famous Negro Artists: Jimi Hendrix/Billie Holiday/Charlie Parker

Draw a **diagram** of the Heart
as arena for gladiators with silver dreams for swords

Knot for sail/ Not for sail/ Not for s**a**le/ Wild card in Dealer's hand

If Onion Gum makes your **mouth** taste like Onions
what makes the brain **feel** Heroic

Funny bone not Humerus

Watch **for** falling stars

CROWN//WARHOL//CROWN

What becomes a Legend most?
   Famous young corpse   shoulder
                                 bicep
Got the Fixin to Die Blues   elbow
                           needle
   GRRR/Clenched teeth/GRRR   forearm
                             hand
Diagram of the Heart pumping Heroin

Beat with a bone to Primitive Rhythms*

Riding with Death *i* spills my heart like **hot coffee**

GRRR/SAMO© IS/ GONE BEYOND WORDS

Never Learned to Repel Ghosts

AN IDEA OF IMPROVISATION IN DUPONT CIRCLE

a DJ Reneg8d remix

A "Blackbird" flies
from a battered sax
at the tonal center
of the circle,
its darkness tipping
the fountain's waves,
rippling flag-like
under an April sky
with a rhythm
striped black and white,
tho perchance
only we can C
what is sigil in its rites.
Ignore the bystanders
assuming the white fountain
can't be metaphor,
or the soaring "Blackbird"
somehow symbol.
Any blue-black wail
over widening water
(even raving evermore)
might feel bound by
simple chords
if what spouted
from the dreadlocked musician
was simply what he'd heard—
but weren't these chords
also voiced by Bird,
whose tarnished horn
wasn't spurred
by splashing water
or rippling wind,
but perhaps a C

sharply diminished
within?
If simply a cerulean sound
of the fountain
stirred or stilled
the green bills in his case,
or solely a white silence
of clouds extended above,
no matter how high,
wouldn't it still be
the yang of water
only brighter?
Why then did he seem
to reed of a thing
more jet than the yen
of a blackbird's
undulating wings on the wind?
Is what the wind
seems to sculpt
more art
or artifact?
Could any sculpture
ringed with purring pigeons
B more than just
a spouting place where he
(god with a minor G)
came to create?
What chords are these?
Which key?
An *i* nearly illusive
as the eye
of Stevens' blackbird
looks to unravel its complex roots,
(but finds merely
real chords it can knot).
And as he blows

this epistle of Paul's
—to augment or diminish
any tint of that sky—
what becomes artifact
in our bicameral minds?
Given how A minor seventh
"singing" of darkness
rings of paradox
in such admiral circles,
could "these broken wings"
provide any lift?
Meaning listen,
who can say
what the "sunken eyes"
of our enslaved ancestors
dreamt of darkly
thinking overboard
of some minor sea?
Oh play black Bird,
riff on if
Si'l vous plait,
these riddle passages
were composed
of changes you chose
and by choosing
tried to unchain.
Contrafact what
—as the conductor
of dusk donned
his onyx tuxedo—
might've swung
in the traffic's rhythm
and why we—
despite knowing
a dominant chord
can't be conflated

with a universal key—
could've begun to sense
in a **siren circling**
above the basin
—above even
the arc & spume
of its spray—
a higher harmony,
not quite
a **Call to Prayer**—
yet nearly glaring
as the small i
of "Arise" . . .

AN IDEA OF IMPROVISATION WITH THE I IN PARADOX

Once, Pythagoras
(my purple plush toy)
hummed joyful sounds
only I could hear
until metal teeth
on the sprocket of logic
severed his single horn.
Newly numb and seeking
to sew together his song,
I took up the trumpet.
Assuming no **mistranslation**,
didn't Pythagoras praise music
as sacred math—
numbers raised to the highest power?
Here I could note how
the throats of birds
tend to angle when raising
the seeds of melody
in their beaks.
Was this how
my school trumpet
angled to be muted
as moonlight flooded
our shoebox apartment
and I practiced
what beauty was aloud?
I believe Pythagoras
could've allowed for the *i*
in lyric as sine of
an imaginary unit.
Perhaps the bird part of our brains
co-signed the seeds of language
by angling our tangents
towards **evergreen** musing about music.

Can't the need inside
a pine or phonograph needle
equally sow air into scents of song?
Have you ever smelled oil
on a trumpet's breath
or felt rhythm uncoil
to kill time around midnight?
Logicians might prove that death
has many fugues—tho little logic—
since death was once branded
with the fugitive logo of the *fleur de lis*.
I swear my boy T claims this
may be the truest thing about beauty:
a lyric can be a useful essay,
but an essay is a useless-ass lyric.
When I play the lyre, I claim
to see lyrics collecting on lips
as dew collects on dogwood leaves.
But do I? Maybe,
I only took up the horn
to learn how to hold Apophenia
and collect her breath
in the bowl of my collar bone.
After an errant elbow
freed some front teeth,
i tried to pick up the horn again,
but red graffiti scrawled
in a school bathroom stall
claimed a one armed man
could never play the violin.
What trumpeter's mouth
isn't an unread wound?
Have you heard how
Lee Morgan could read sheet music
easily as his Beloved's grocery notes,
but still misread her most notable longing?

There are some nights I think
Pythagoras merely saw music
as the grammar of sound making sentences,
but listen—who among us hasn't needed
to number the hoarse notes
galloping out of a bridled mouth?

THE RUMI IN YOU

stirs to wonder—
what bruise could ruin love
more than the rasp
of eroding rain?
When I say rasp
you may think of rust,
another type of ruin
related to rain.
Did you not grasp
how Jalaluddin
was among the Last Poets
whose nappy beard
faced ruin in every nation
including rumination?
As one Harvest moon
acquired a goatee of clouds,
didn't you almost admit
to whiskering a weak chin
as if your own ruined beauty
was an unwearable thing?
Although you've seldom
whispered it, *wabi-sabi*—
Japanese for the reign of ruin—
could be a Rumi word.
When you first heard
the flamenco of ruin
begin to flower,
did you lament
or invent a belief
in *wabi-sabi*?
Could such belief
in lonely bruising
begin a diction
to the long open you

found in "wound"
or say why that *i*
so central to your **faith**
ran quietly as a letter
left out in the rain?
Perhaps outside some window
you misheard **wind**
blown petals whispering*
"Rein in mystery."
As you once saw
a bruise begin to whisk
a thickening roux
from a flower's fat sorrow,
couldn't your beard
have also masqueraded
as faith or masculinity
or perhaps even a beloved
which blooms
through dark whiskers
until you start to hear
how some poets become lovers
of the sound of **rain**,
but others simply lovers
of the sound of ruin?

ACKNOWLEDGEMENTS

This manuscript has been more than two decades in the making, thus it might be impossible for me to thank everyone. Apologies in advance to anyone I may miss. Please know it was inadvertent. First thanks goes to my mother Anna Santos Dias Porter without whom I wouldn't be here. All I ever wanted to do was make you proud. Thanks for understanding that I was a born creative and giving me permission to be who I am. I can't imagine how difficult it must have been to raise two kids, one of whom was an undiagnosed boy on the autism spectrum. Extra special thanks to Kwoya Fagin Maples, Terrance Hayes, Jeffery McDaniel, and Emari DiGiorgio for reading this manuscript and providing their invaluable insight. I have been blessed with many lifelong friends, but Kenneth Carroll gets at least half the credit for anything I have done or will do. I could never repay him (and his family) for basically adopting me and for being the best mentor any writer could ever hope to have. Without Kenny I would likely not know any of the people I am about to thank. Shout out to Brian Gilmore for being not only a great friend but for keeping me in check all these years. Extra special shout out to Yona Harvey and Terrance Hayes for being everything, everything, but first and foremost for putting up with a brother's quirks and oddities for 25+ years. I love both of you more than words could ever say. Thanks to Jeffrey McDaniel for being a friend and editor. Thanks to Ed Ochester for considering my manuscript. Shout out to my fellow Black Roosters: Gary Lilley, Brandon D. Johnson, and the brilliant Ernesto Mercer. Shout out to Tyehimba Jess, A. Van Jordan, Jericho Brown, Herman Beavers, and John Murillo for letting me peep your manuscripts back in the day and along the way. Shout out to Toi Derricotte and Cornelius Eady for creating Cave Canem and letting a kid from the projects with no college feel like he belonged. Shout out to Afaa Michael Weaver and Elizabeth Alexander for believing in me way back when and to all the individual amazing CC Fellows. Shout out to Nicole Sealey and Elizabeth Bryant for all their hard work. Shout out to Sharan Strange and Thomas Sayers Ellis and the Dark Room Collective. Shout out to Dr. Joanne Gabbin and Furious Flower. Shout out to poets who found time to help a young poet, especially Sonia Sanchez, Amiri Baraka, Yusef Komunyakaa, Lucille Clifton, Laini Mataka, Gaston Neal, Carolyn Forchè, and Henry Taylor. I was blessed to meet so many awesome people living in DC, shout out to DJ Kool, for teaching me how to be a committed craftsman, shout out to Simba and Yao and extra special thanks for "4,000 Shades of Blue" & "LibationSong" and for letting me be part of the Karibu Books crew, shout out to Toni Asante Lightfoot and the poets of the M.U.G., shout out to The POEMCEEs and It's Your Mug, Kaffa House and Mangos. Shout out to M'Wile Askari and Kwelismith, to Reuben Jackson and Jennifer Smith, to the WritersCorps crew with a special shout out to Joe Ray Sandoval. Shout out to my Howard University crew; Yona, Ta-Nehisi, Jelani Cobb, Sarasvati A. Lewis, Toni Blackman, Yaphet Brinson, and Natalie Hopkinson. Shout out to Tony Medina, to Alan & Derrick & Fred, to Darry Strickland and Sami Miranda. Shout out to the South Jersey Poets, to Peter Murphy and Murphy Writing of Stockton University, Aubrey Rahab, Emily Van Duyne, and especially to Emari DiGiorgio. Shout out to Michael Onyeagoro and Lisa Romaine. Many of these poems and my evolution as a poet and a person would not be possible without Gigi Sturdivant, to whom I am forever indebted. Shout out to my amazing family, especially Derri Dias, and Austin McCloud. Shout out to Prince Rogers Nelson for making space for weird black bays to be who they truly were. Last and not least, shout out to my amazing son Joel Crooms-Porter, your Daddy loves you. Gracious thanks to everyone who ever sat in a classroom while Mr. Dias-Porter rambled on endlessly in too much detail about whatever. Last and most def not least shout out to Andrea Walls and Marissa Johnson-Valenzuela at Thread Makes Blanket press for making this book happen.

Gracious thanks all the magazines and journals where versions of these poems have been previously published and which include;

"Wednesday Poem," *The New York Times*

"Idea of Improvisation with the Uncertainty Principle–Take X," *Southern Indiana Review*

"Three Wrong Notes," *Poem-A-Day*

"El Magnifico," *Callaloo*

"Subterranean Night-colored Magi," appeared in *Asheville Poetry Review, HyperAge, Obsidian II,* and *Poetry Nation.* It also appeared in the movie *Slam.*

"Landscape," first appeared in *G.W. Review.* It was also included in *360 Degrees—A Revolution of Black Poetry.*

"Still Life," *Articulate*

"Morna," *Cimboa*

"Monday," and "Irony of a Negro Artist," were included in the *Black Rooster Anthology.*

"Father, Son, Wholly Ghost," *Cave Canem I*

"Portrait of the Artist as a Starfish in Coffee", "Turning the Tables", and "Notched in the Bow of a Wave," *Poetry*

"A Solo for LaSon" and "A Love Supreme," *Beltway Quarterly*

"Elegy Indigo," *Brilliant Corners.* It was also included in *Best American Poetry 2014*

"Music Lessons," *Bridge 8*

"Psychopharmacologia," *Mead*

"Whitman's Sampler", "The Idea Of Improvisation at Newport '61", "The Al Kwarizmi in You," *Black Renaissance Noir*

"The Basho in You", "The Bukowski in You", "The Coltrane in You", "Grammar Note" under the title "Grammar Lesson": The Journal of Bahá'í Studies

The section headers were previously published as "An Idea of Improvisation as the I in Paradox" (now the title of a different poem in this book) in *Phi Kappa Phi Forum Magazine.*

NOTES

Within each poem, the maroon text can be read as its own poem. Most of these ghost poems are Japanese short forms.

"An Idea of Improvisation as the I in Kaleidoscope"
   is the title for the section headers which can be read as comprising a triptych.

"Rap 23"
   is a translation of the 23rd Psalms into African American Vernacular.

"Whitman's Sampler"
   is a cento of lines from Walt Whitman poems. The symbol "i" is used in engineering contexts to denote an electrical current and is also used in mathematical contexts to denote the square root of negative one or the Imaginary Unit of Complex Numbers (a type of multitude.) Thus the symbol i can be understood in this poem to both sing the body electric and signify that it contains multitudes.

"An Idea of Improvisation with the Uncertainty Principle—Take X"
   * light breeze—what troubles this body of water

"Elegy Indigo"
   is a Bop and the refrain is from "Open Heart" by Sekou Sundiata.

"*Ideias di Improvison na Porto Ingles*"
   "*Pasarinhu ki komi pimenta sabi kel ku ki ten*" loosely translates as "a bird that eats (hot) peppers knows what kind of anus they'll have" *midjo o nonsi* is meal or flour, *oril* is a game played in many West African countries, and "*Konbersa sabe e ladron di tempu*" means "A good conversation is a thief of time"

"An Idea of Improvisation as Morna"
   Sao Vicente, Santiago, Fogo, Sao Nicolau, Sal, Maio, Boavista, Santa Luzia, and Brava comprise the Cape Verde Islands

txuba is rain (also means hope), *badiu* are rural peasants, *Kriolu* is
Portuguese Creole, and *koladera* is fast paced dance music

"An Idea of Improvisation with Violin"
Elijah Jovan McCain was a 23-year-old Black American massage therapist
who often played his violin at a local animal shelter to help soothe the
animals. On the night of August 24th, 2019 he was stopped while walking
and killed by the Aurora Colorado Police Department. An independent
investigation commissioned by the Aurora City Council found that the
police had no legal basis for stopping, frisking, or restraining McClain
or for asking paramedics to inject him with ketamine while he was
already restrained. Although police claimed that their body cameras
were knocked off during a struggle with McClain the audio still captured
McClain's final words: "Oh, I'm sorry, I wasn't trying to do that. I just can't
breathe correctly."

"Still Life"
1. grammar note: The blood of a black boy lays in the street—it does not
lie.

"An Idea Of Improvisation With The Table Of Contents of *The Human Hours*"
This is a found poem using the actual table of contents from The Human
Hours: Poems by Catharine Barnett, with the order of a few of the titles
slightly altered for mostly musical purposes.

"Seascape with Vessel"
Some of the Kriolu words are also Cesaria Evora song titles
sodade is a mix of nostalgia and homesickness, *txintxirote* is a type of
seabird, *frutu proibido* is forbidden fruit, *destino negro* means negro
destiny, *coragem irmon* means courage brother, *consedjo* is advice,
counsel, *morabeza* means welcome, and *despidida* means farewell

"Sometimes It Snows In April"
is a Quotilla and the first word of each line forms the phrase "April is the
cruelest month breeding lilacs out of the dead land."

"An Idea of Improvisation at Newport"
    is a partial Quotilla and the first word of each phrase in the middle
    section forms the sentence "Raindrops on roses and whiskers on
    kittens" "Hafez" is a reference to both the Sufi Poet Hafez of Shiraz
    and the ethnomusicologist Hafez Modirzadeh who wrote "Aural
    Archetypes and Cyclic Perspectives in the Work of John Coltrane and
    Ancient Chinese Music Theory"

"An Idea of Improvisation with the Uncertainty Principle—Take Y"
    * a single leaf swirling through the garden—the mailman

"Algorithm of the Blues"
    The song "Ornithology" is a contrafact of the song "How High the
    Moon". This poem references Joy Harjo and incorporates several phrases
    from poems dedicated to Charlie Parker which appear in "The Jazz
    Anthology".

"The Man with the [12 Bar] Blues Guitar"
    What if I were gone, and the wind still reeks of hyacinth, what then.
    —Lucie Brock-Broido

"A Theory of Lyric"
    The chemical symbol for chromium is Cr, oxygen is O, and tungsten is W.

"Irony of a Negro Artist"
    * slave quarters—every cabin a master bedroom

"An Idea of Improvisation at Dupont Circle"
    makes reference to several Wallace Stevens poems and also employs
    a few words and many of the chords from the progression of the
    Beatles song "Blackbird" (G Am7 C C#dim) sounded out as language.

"The Rumi in You"
    * so many reflections—this little stream of consciousness